Baby Wea

Parent's Guide to Successfully Weaning Their Baby Towards Solid Foods and Raising a Healthy, Happy and Self-Assured Child

By Laura Nicol

© **Copyright 2020 - All rights reserved.**

The content contained within this book may not be reproduced, duplicated or transmitted without direct written permission from the author or the publisher.

Under no circumstances will any blame or legal responsibility be held against the publisher or author for any damages, reparation, or monetary loss due to the information contained within this book. Either directly or indirectly.

Legal Notice:

This book is copyright protected. This book is only for personal use. You cannot amend, distribute, sell, use, quote or paraphrase any part, or the content within this book, without the consent of the author or publisher.

Disclaimer Notice:

Please note the information contained within this document is for educational and entertainment purposes only. All effort has been executed to present accurate, up to date and reliable, complete information. No warranties of any kind are declared or implied. Readers acknowledge that the author is not engaging in the rendering of legal, financial, medical or professional advice. The content within this book has been derived from various sources. Please consult a licensed professional before attempting any techniques outlined in this book.

By reading this document, the reader agrees that under no

circumstances is the author responsible for any losses, direct or indirect, which are incurred as a result of the use of information contained within this document, including, but not limited to, —errors, omissions, or inaccuracies.

Contents

Chapter 1: When Should You Wean Your Baby 7

Chapter 2: Baby Weaning Resources 10

Chapter 3: Baby Weaning Misconceptions 13

   # 1: 6 Months Is the Time 13

   # 2: Breastfeeding Lasts Too Long 14

   # 3: Weaning Is Too Tough 14

Chapter 4: Get Going With Baby Weaning 16

   # 1: Skipping A Feeding 16

   # 2: Older Kids Can Postpone 17

   # 3: Shorten the Time 17

Chapter 5: How to Make Weaning Easier 19

Chapter 6: Allowing Your Kid to Wean Naturally 22

Chapter 7: Which Age Is Too Old to Breastfeed? 25

   What To Do 25

Chapter 8: Adding Cuddle Time 28

Chapter 9: Meal by Meal 31

   Choose A Meal 31

   Next Up 32

Chapter 10: Prolonged Breastfeeding Advantages 34

Chapter 11: How to Get Started 37

   Action 1: Identify If Your Kid Is Ready 37

   Action 2: Maintain Security 38

   Action 3: Maintain Positivity 38

   Step 4: Urge Daddy To Get Involved 39

Step 5: Know That Nights Are Hardest 39
Chapter 12: Handling Other People's Advice 40
Chapter 13: Transitioning From Breast Milk To A Cup 43
Chapter 14: Medical Reasons For Baby Weaning 46
    Can Something Else Be Done? 46
Chapter 15: Why Stopping Abruptly is a Bad Idea 49
Chapter 16: Baby Weaning Process 52
    Introducing The Process 52
    Completing The Process 53
Chapter 17: Time for Night Weaning 55
Chapter 18: Tips For Natural Weaning 58
Chapter 19: Night Weaning 61
    # 1: Slow and Steady Wins The Race 61
    # 2: Increase the Length 62
    # 3: Provide The Kid With More Throughout The Day 62
Chapter 20: Weaning A Toddler If a Brand-new One Is On The Way 64
Chapter 21: What Happens When You Stop Breastfeeding? 67
Chapter 22: Baby Weaning Explained 70
    Why Is It Difficult? 70
    What To Do 71
Chapter 23: Why is Weaning Hard? 73
Chapter 24: When To Baby Wean 76
Chapter 25: When To Night Wean 79

Thank you for buying this book and I hope that you will find it useful. If you will want to share your thoughts on this book, you can do so by leaving a review on the Amazon page, it helps me out a lot.

Chapter 1: When Should You Wean Your Baby

When to you wean a baby? There are several theories on this, and it could be among the most frequently posed questions. Even they might not have the ability to tell you when the procedure ought to be begun. The truth is, numerous moms require a clear answer that tells them when they ought to simply stop. One such answer doesn't exist. The truth is, it requires a good deal of time to make this baby weaning procedure occur, and nobody can tell you when to stop.

In the USA, it is approximated that just around 20 percent of babies are still nursing at 6 months old. This is an extremely low number. When you contrast this to most other countries, you might discover that the distinctions are rather striking. For instance, in many European, African and Asian cultures, babies are going to breastfeed up until they are between 2 and 4 years old. A number of moms in these nations would see stopping breastfeeding so young, as is performed in the USA by the majority of moms, as really wrong.

Why keep going, or why stop? There's no proof that there is any damage to a kid that is breastfed longer. There are lots of advantages to breastfeeding longer. You are going to discover that the kid is obtaining the nutrition it requires. You are going to additionally see that even if you breastfeed your kid simply once a day, there is an advantage in this. Culturally, individuals in the USA have actually put a black mark on the procedure of breastfeeding past a couple of months; however, this does not need to be the instance.

As a parent, remember why you decided to breastfeed, to begin with. The nutrition is perfect for the kid. The bond which forms in between the baby and you is extremely powerful. Most significantly, you have actually established a kid which has come to view breastfeeding as a procedure which maintains them comfy and safe.

The procedure of baby weaning is one that has no time restriction. Consider what is proper for your kid independently instead of searching for a goal beyond this. Eventually, you ought to motivate your kid to decide by seeing what he/she requires instead of listening to what your buddy has actually told you is suitable for them.

Chapter 2: Baby Weaning Resources

When it pertains to baby weaning, everybody has a viewpoint. You are going to discover women with no experience providing recommendations on the length of time a baby ought to breastfeed. You might even discover that everybody you know has a distinct opinion regarding when the baby ought to stop breastfeeding. While this prevails, it is necessary to keep in mind that it is extremely crucial to make this decision on your own, based upon what you and your baby require from the procedure. Nevertheless, where can you go for help?

First off, among the ideal places to get assistance from is your pediatrician. Your pediatrician ought to be somebody who you trust with your kid's health, and if you do not, you ought to be trying to find another professional to assist you. The truth is, you want to have an excellent idea of what your kid requires at this moment in time, regardless of how old they are. Speak with your medical professional about your kid and breastfeeding. Because babies do see their physicians frequently, this is a concern you can discuss whenever you feel it is suitable. The

American Academy of Paediatrics advises that babies are breastfed up until they are at least one year of age. However, that does not indicate your medical professional is going to suggest this.

Aside from your pediatrician, who understands the well being and health of your kid, there are numerous other locations to get information and guidance on breastfeeding. You might want to keep away from those who might not have a viewpoint which is based upon facts. For instance, in case a friend who has actually never ever breastfed has an opinion, it is not originating from experience. Stay clear of these and speak with somebody that has actually breastfed and learn how they resolved the procedure. You can discover a range of excellent support groups available on the web, as well. This could be a wonderful resource for moms who desire impartial viewpoints on when they ought to think about baby weaning. Remember that it is your decision.

Baby weaning is a procedure which is not simply specified by when you ought to stop breastfeeding, yet additionally by how to do so. You are going to discover the procedure more satisfying after you have actually collected information and facts from trustworthy sources.

Chapter 3: Baby Weaning Misconceptions

Weaning babies is a procedure in which a kid stops breastfeeding from their mom and moves to consuming nothing except solid foods or a from a bottle. This procedure is eventual, and there is no established time table for when it ought to occur. This is particularly true because the majority of babies need to make up their minds by themselves. Each is distinct. Their requirements, both physically and mentally, are distinct. Because breastfeeding is a lot more than feedings, it is very crucial to think about all sides of the procedure. When it concerns baby weaning, there are typically numerous misconceptions. Here are 3 to remember.

1: 6 Months Is the Time

Among the worst mistakes you could make is to presume that your kid needs to be weaned by the time they are 6 months old. Actually, the American Academy of Paediatrics advises that moms keep on breastfeeding their kids up until at least the age of one. Worldwide, stopping breastfeeding before a kid's 2nd birthday is weird. It is actually a decision that the kid has to make. Are they prepared for the shift? If not, they are going to let you know. It is difficult to push a kid just like that.

2: Breastfeeding Lasts Too Long

The truth is, there is no reason to stop breastfeeding early. Numerous kids wish to continue with breastfeeding for one reason or another and ought to be permitted to do so. They ought to be place onto solid foods by the age of 6 months, however, they could supplement this with breastfeeding for a few more years without an issue. Breast milk is extremely healthy during a kid's initial years. It could assist to shield their immunity and permits the body to develop appropriately.

3: Weaning Is Too Tough

The procedure of weaning a kid from the breast is one which does require time. The quantity of time it requires actually depends upon the kid. If a kid hesitates to stop breastfeeding, there is probably a reason why this is occurring. In this instance, speak with the kid's pediatrician and make sure to work with the kid to comprehend why.

In numerous circumstances, individuals have a mistaken belief about why moms pick to breastfeed for more than a year. The point is that there is absolutely nothing amiss with the procedure. It does not impact the growth of a kid adversely but does promote a potent immunity.

Chapter 4: Get Going With Baby Weaning

You have chosen that your kid has to be weaned. Now what? There are various techniques for weaning your baby off of breast milk. You could consider all of them as feasible choices, as long as they do work for you. Not everything is going to work, however. The first thing you want to do is to make certain your kid is prepared. To do this, ensure they are sufficiently enough and obtaining sufficient calories from the food they are ingesting. If so, consider these 3 techniques.

1: Skipping A Feeding

Possibly the easiest of techniques is just skipping a feeding. Simply do not do breastfeeding and see how your kid responds. As an alternative to breastfeeding, provide a cup of breast milk or formula. This is maybe among the ideal methods because you are just going to carry out a feeding once every week or so. Over the following couple of weeks, not just is the kid going to adjust to this, the body will adjust too.

2: Older Kids Can Postpone

If your kid is sufficiently old to speak with, divert them throughout the times when you would usually breastfeed them. Rather than really going to sit and breastfeed, take the kid outside for a walk at that time. By doing this, the kid has something to take up his time. If the kid does request breastfeeding, allow them to know you are going to do that later on. Divert them from it.

3: Shorten the Time

The last technique of weaning enables the breastfeeding mom to shorten the quantity of time that the kid is nursing. Make certain the kid is obtaining all of the food he/she requires from other source, like a healthy treat. Then, gradually cut down on the quantity of time they are breastfeeding. Go from 5 minutes to 3 minutes, down to 2, and so forth. Feedings ought to dwindle. If you are doing this with a kid that is under 6 months of age, it is necessary to change to a bottle-feeding schedule to ensure that no nutrients are lacking.

These 3 approaches are just 3 choices. There are a lot of other techniques out there, as well. The objective you ought to have is weaning your baby gradually so that there is no abrupt stopping, which could impact them mentally. When you achieve this, you and the kid are going to be on a course to enhance their capability to quit breastfeeding and your capability to quit fretting about it.

Chapter 5: How to Make Weaning Easier

The weaning procedure could be challenging, and it can frequently leave both mom and kid wanting a couple more months (or longer) of the procedure. When the time has actually come to wean your kid from breastfeeding, it could be fantastic. If you put in the time to make it a great step in the appropriate direction, everybody is going to gain from it. Here are certain pointers to assist you in making weaning simpler.

1. When you would generally be nursing, introduce your kid to anything which is enjoyable or brand-new to them. Even better, take them outdoors to play throughout this time. They are not even going to consider breastfeeding if you occupy them sufficiently throughout this time.

2. Do not wear the clothes that you generally put on while nursing. This keeps the breastfeeding signal away from the mind. Rather than sitting in your regular nursing area, select other locations in the room to sit. Once again, it busts the connection.

3. For kids that are younger than a year, you are going to probably be substituting a breastfeeding session with a bottle or often a cup. Do so when you would usually be feeding the kid. This permits the kid to associate the procedure of breastfeeding with the bottle.

4. For kids who are older than a year, you are going to want to be a tad more imaginative in selecting something to fill this time. Rather than breastfeeding, encourage a healthy treat. Alternatively, you might wish to skip the food entirely and simply plan a bit of time to snuggle together.

5. Ensure there are diversions when typical breastfeeding times are. Daddy can assist here. Encourage daddy to hang around doing something exciting with the kid throughout this time.

6. Do not wean them as they are teething or if there is another change taking place in their lives. You do not wish for them to be mentally scarred by the

occasion! Let them adjust to other changes initially, and then present the weaning procedure.

7. Notice that your kid might get another calming habit, like sucking a thumb or hanging on to a blanket. This ought to be fine and not dissuaded because they are merely trying to find safety from it. Let them make a psychological break such as this.

Promoting breastfeeding throughout any of these circumstances should not be done. By taking these actions, you could securely assist your kid in shifting far from breastfeeding.

Chapter 6: Allowing Your Kid to Wean Naturally

The American Academy of Paediatrics suggests that infants are not pushed to wean whatsoever. They additionally advise that a mom breastfeeds for at least a complete year. The WHO has a distinct view. They encourage kids to breastfeed up until they are 2 years of age. Still, there is no limitation to when you need to stop, and there is definitely no reason to do so prior to the kid being prepared to do so. You ought to enable your kid to wean off breastfeeding when it is natural for them to do so.

Let your kid decide when to breastfeed. Many babies are going to stop breastfeeding between the ages of 12 months and 18 months; however, others might take a bit more to be prepared to do so. What are a few of the advantages of this natural process? Have these in mind.

- In case the baby graduates to more solid foods and is alright with missing their breastfeeding session, let it be. This reveals that they are self-assured and no longer require the safety of your breast to let the procedure of feeding take place.

- Enable your kid to breastfeed longer, and you could skip the bottle requirement completely. Numerous kids go from breastfeeding straight to drinking liquids out of a cup. They do not have to spend plenty of nights having a tough time with a bottle then. You get to skip the expense of the bottles as well.

- Allow the kid to figure out when to cease breastfeeding, and you will not need to undergo the withdrawal of the procedure. As they naturally substitute their meals from the breast with meals from the table, they are going to get accustomed to the procedure. So are you. Numerous moms struggle with this procedure due to the fact that it could be extremely confining to understand that your kid is breastfeeding no more.

Take the procedure one action at a time. They might be piqued by a brand-new taste for breakfast and might feel much better about eating what their sister or brother is. The majority of kids are able to breastfeed properly past the age of one without an issue. When you let them stop breastfeeding naturally, you both emerge as winners. They stay away from much of the risks kids who are fed face. Plus, they are more comfy with the shift if they are part of the shift to quit breastfeeding. You might discover that this allows you to be more happy to stop, as well.

Chapter 7: Which Age Is Too Old to Breastfeed?

There are numerous views on the subject of breastfeeding in regards to when you ought to stop it. Eventually, this is a choice that ought to be made by you and your kid, however, there arrives a time when every kid needs to make the break from breastfeeding and begin concentrating on a more adult eating plan. The concern is when. There are numerous things to remember when enabling your kid to carry on breastfeeding beyond the age of one. In the USA, this is taken into consideration as regular, however, in many other nations, kids up to the age of 4 are going to breastfeed. Having this in mind, you are going to want to create some strategies and changes.

What To Do

If your kid is not yet all set to cease breastfeeding, there is no reason to stop them from doing that, presuming they are younger than the age of 4. Throughout this time, however, you are going to wish to move far from the consistent breastfeeding and utilize it more as an occasional reward. It is vital to bear in mind that a kid at the age of 6 months ought to be beginning to consume solid food. Healthwise, they have to be taking in solid food in stages beginning at 6 months. After this, the majority of their calories ought to be originating from food, not breastfeeding. This additionally permits them not to require to nurse to sustain themselves continuously.

Throughout this time, it could additionally be suitable to provide your kid with breast milk. They do not have to breastfeed to obtain this milk, however. You could put it in their cereal and other foods. They could additionally consume it in a cup. It is suitable to do this up through preschool, in case you feel it is necessary to do so. They must not be dependant on breast milk for nutrition, however.

Ultimately, you are going to want to make the break from breastfeeding absolutely. It is frequently essential to bear in mind that kids can breastfeed too long. Those that do might have a greater hesitation to stop. Instead of permitting this, a mom has to make certain that the kid is mentally steady and entirely well-fed beyond breastfeeding. Make certain to speak with your pediatrician in case you feel that your kid is having a problem with any facet of weaning or if you are uncertain how to go towards the procedure with your kid.

Chapter 8: Adding Cuddle Time

Baby weaning is the procedure of making it possible for a baby to quit breastfeeding and rathrt to work towards consuming either from a bottle, if the kid is younger, or from a cup and consuming solid foods. The time frame for performing this is actually up to the mom and the kid as natural baby weaning ought to constantly be the parent's objective. Yet, when the time arrives to begin working towards weaning, you might wish to think about why the kid is resisting. It might be that they are hungry, which indicates changing their meals to include additional calories. For lots of other kids, the requirement to breastfeed is not about eating, it is about time with mommy.

There is a great deal of bonding which takes place between a mom and her kid throughout the breastfeeding experience. This bond is what makes it possible for the kid to be comfy and feel protected as it is young and growing. Ultimately, there is going to arrive a time when the kid has to quit breastfeeding, however, an issue can occur where the kid is less happy to do so since they yearn for and, actually, require this intimate time with their parents. The bright side is that you could aid them through this procedure effectively.

It is essential to think about baby weaning with regard to psychological strength. Urging babies to wean typically indicates still providing that close bonding time they require. Only mommy is going to do in numerous circumstances, however, daddy ought to feel like part of the procedure as well. For instance, given that the kid requires that close proximity, it might be an excellent idea to devote a bit of time every day to snuggling instead of nursing. For instance, maybe your kid nurses every day at 11 am. You have actually fed them solid foods, and you are now sitting down to spend a bit of time enjoying a favorite tv program. Snuggle with them at this time. They have a full stomach and simply require the sensation of security which typically accompanies breastfeeding. With a bit of snuggle time, however, they could quit breastfeeding without losing that required security.

As you could see, the breastfeeding procedure is one which integrates a vast array of various things. You are going to want to satisfy the kid's physical requirements of consuming ample calories.

However, you additionally need to think about the kid's requirement for comfort and security. When you can satisfy both of these requirements, everybody involved is going to be in a better place.

Chapter 9: Meal by Meal

There are lots of methods to encourage baby weaning to occur. There comes a time when you have to make the initial move, however. If it is time to think about baby weaning, you might wish to do the procedure one action at a time. More properly, you wish to do the procedure meal by meal. Doing so could assist you and your kid to do properly in regard to handling the procedure. If you are prepared to begin weaning, think about the one meal at a time technique to help with that.

Choose A Meal

The initial step is to select a particular meal to begin with. Pick a meal you are most comfy with quitting initially. There is no particular requirement regarding which meal to work with. The objective is simply to pick one which works ideally for you. As soon as you understand which one it is going to be, stop breastfeeding at this meal. Rather, add in a healthy solid food meal for the kid. Based upon the age of the kid, you might want to overcome the steps of offering a baby solid food consisting of selecting cereals initially, and after that, veggies and fruits, etc. If the kid is currently consuming solid foods, you are going to simply substitute one of his/her meals at the breast with solid foods.

Next Up

Keep this up for a week at least. You do not wish to cut the kid off from breastfeeding too rapidly as this could induce the kid to deal with a variety of various sensations, consisting of psychological loss. Rather, every day for the following week, feed the kid that identical meal in solid foods. Do not sit in the identical area you have actually sat for breastfeeding, as well.

When this has actually been successful for a complete week, you could make the shift to the following meal. Choose the following regular breastfeeding and skip it by substituting it with a healthier meal for the kid. Once again, it matters not which meal it is, as much as it matters how you go through the procedure. You are just substituting the 2nd meal at the breast with a meal at the table.

Keep on doing this, permitting a complete week between every shift. You are going to discover some resistance along the way, however, in many cases, the procedure is going to be successful. Go slowly and work at a rate proper for baby and you.

Chapter 10: Prolonged Breastfeeding Advantages

For those moms who are not sure of whether they ought to go through the procedure of baby weaning just yet, think about a few of the advantages of prolonged breastfeeding, or breastfeeding your kid past the age of 6 months. Keep in mind to have an open mind when it pertains to thinking about when you ought to wean the baby from breastfeeding. It ought to be a choice left up to your baby when he/she is lastly comfy to let the breastfeeding go and prefers all solid foods instead.

While not all moms have to utilize prolonged breastfeeding, for some, it looks like what the kid desires. There is absolutely nothing bad about feeding your kid by breast more than what is seen as average. Rather, think about a few of the advantages of the procedure.

1. Breastfeeding offers your baby the advantages that extend to the immunity. To put it simply, they obtain the immunological benefits which naturally

originate from drinking human-made milk. As a kid is simply a couple of months old, this advantage could aid them to stay healthy longer and to fight off a lot of the infections kids catch. Toddlers are healthier in case they breastfeed longer.

2. Lots of babies sense that breastfeeding is more than a food source. It is additionally the location to go when they require comfort from mommy. When they are afraid, dismayed about something, or just hurt, this is among the ideal methods to assist the kid in boosting their feelings.

3. You stay clear of much of the typical problems related to non-human milk, particularly allergy symptoms. Lots of kids can additionally gain from the rewards of lower cancer risk from breastfeeding for a longer period of time.

Possibly the greatest advantage to extended breastfeeding is merely helping the kid with deciding on his own. There are a great deal of misunderstandings about the procedure, such as the one that claims the kid is going to end up being too connected to his mom if he breastfeeds for too long. This is just not the instance. Instead, the kid is most probable to be healthier and have a more powerful bond with their parents. Additionally, they get assistance when it comes to deciding to stop, and they are physically and emotionally prepared to do so.

Prolonged breastfeeding is a choice for a lot of parents. There are few, if any, reasons to quit breastfeeding your kid sooner. Actually, you might discover that it is a lot more appropriate to keep at the procedure for a bit longer.

Chapter 11: How to Get Started

Are you prepared to quit breastfeeding your kid? If so, you might be uncertain of where to begin to quit the procedure. Each kid is distinct, and it is extremely crucial for a parent to make the appropriate decision for their kid. To achieve this, it is really crucial to take into consideration if your kid is prepared. Here are certain actions to follow to assist you during baby weaning.

Action 1: Identify If Your Kid Is Ready

A kid under the age of 6 months ought to change to a formula if they are not breastfeeding anymore. A kid who is over 6 months ought to be consuming some solid food. Once they are consuming the majority of their calories from solid food, you can think about switching them to a cup rather than breastfeeding.

Action 2: Maintain Security

As you quit breastfeeding, bear in mind that your kid still requires a great deal of safety. Every week, get rid of one breastfeeding from the schedule. Throughout that time, do things which keep the kid occupied, yet additionally safe and secure and comfy. Snuggle together. Hang out playing together. This maintains them mentally strong through the occasion. Make certain that the kid has the ability to let go like this.

Action 3: Maintain Positivity

Each kid is special when it comes to stopping with feeding on the breast. Some are going to ask for it. Others are never going to hesitate about it. It is ideal to keep the kid who is asking occupied, so there is no worry about the procedure. In case they ask for it, tell them they could breastfeed later on. At the moment, you ought to have something exciting for them to do, as going outdoors to play.

Step 4: Urge Daddy To Get Involved

Now is a good time for daddy to begin assisting with meals and to begin having fun with the baby throughout breastfeeding times. It is frequently essential for daddy to get included in feeding the kid solid foods to ensure that they can break from believing that just mommy supplies this.

Step 5: Know That Nights Are Hardest

Night breastfeeding, as that before bed, is frequently the toughest time to break from. Encourage the kid to read or simply spend time snuggling together. Have a bedtime treat initially.

The procedure ought to be steady. Motivate your kid to breastfeed if it is required. However, work towards breaking the habit gradually. You and your kid are going to value the procedure if you go through it this way.

Chapter 12: Handling Other People's Advice

Numerous families are going to have a couple of individuals inside them that motivate a breastfeeding mom to quit breastfeeding. For certain reason, they think that the procedure ought to stop a lot sooner, and because you are the kid's mom, you are not delighted about their remarks. Besides, don't you know what is ideal for your kid? Lots of households have this kind of occurrence. If you are a breastfeeding mommy, it could aid to have a bit of information and pointers to handle those telling you to quit breastfeeding.

- The American Academy of Paediatricians suggests that kids should be breastfed at least up until they are one year old. There is neither reason nor advantage to quitting before this.

- The WHO urges moms to breastfeed their kids up until the age of 2 years of age. Actually, in numerous nations throughout Europe, Africa, and Asia kids are breastfed up until they are between the ages of 2 and 4 years of age.

- There is no proof that a kid which is breastfed is any less capable of growing. Actually, kids who get the nutrients from breastfeeding, in fact, grow much better and are less vulnerable to disease consisting of all the things from cancer to infections.

- Babies ought to be motivated to quit breastfeeding just when they are prepared o do so. You ought to not feel like this is anything you are doing wrong, specifically considering that it is rather typical and natural for a mom to breastfeed their kid far more than what plenty of folks in the USA do.

- Consider your kid's pediatrician as the ideal best tool in assisting you in deciding to quit breastfeeding. They understand you, and they know your kid. They additionally understand your kid's well being and health. These are the tools required to make the proper decision about when to quit breastfeeding.

Every kid is distinct. Some kids wish to quit breastfeeding a lot sooner. When this holds true, let them do so. There is no reason to force it. However, never ever permit somebody else to tell you when your kid ought to quit being breastfed. The reality is, your kid is going to assist you in making this choice naturally. It is most effective and most useful for the procedure to take place naturally to ensure that the kid and the mom are both ready for it.

Chapter 13: Transitioning From Breast Milk To A Cup

As you begin thinking about quitting to breastfeed your baby, you might be questioning how you are going to get them to avoid the bottle and go straight to the cup. There is truly no reason to need to place a breastfeed baby onto a bottle unless you are stopping them from all breastfeeding prior to the age of one. In this situation, it might be essential to think about the requirement for a bottle for a couple of months, or up until their physician advises that they no longer require a bottle whatsoever.

The initial step in making the shift from breastfeeding to the cup is to begin introducing the cup into their everyday lives. For instance, when the kid is in between 6 months and 9 months of age, the kid might have the ability to utilize a sip cup where they are ingesting a couple of ounces of breast milk, water or juice every day. Provide this to them during the day to assist satiate their thirst instead of feeding them. These cups must not meddle with their feedings. In case they do, the kid is obtaining too many.

For the following couple of months, carry on utilizing the sippy cup. As you bring in increasingly more solid foods into the kid's eating plan, enable them to stop breastfeeding throughout the day. Enable them to consume breast milk, if you want, out of a sippy cup during the day with their solid food meals. This is going to depend, once again, on the age of the kid, however, many kids by the age of 9 months ought to be eating solid food. Work towards your pediatrician's objectives here, however. Carry on breastfeeding during the night, like right prior to bed. This makes it possible for that convenience and security to be offered to the kid.

As you go towards the end outcome, keep enabling the kid to wean from the breast naturally. You wish to permit this procedure to work up until it is most comfy for the kid to quit breastfeeding. For instance, your kid might wish to quit breastfeeding entirely due to the fact that he wishes to enjoy a film with his bro or sis rather than resting on mommy's lap.

When you enable this procedure to occur as naturally as feasible, you are going to discover that it is satisfying to both them and you. Additionally, it enables them to avoid needing to utilize a bottle entirely. This procedure is an outstanding advantage for every individual included.

Chapter 14: Medical Reasons For Baby Weaning

There are circumstances when it might end up being required for a person to quit breastfeeding for medical purposes. For instance, if you and your kid have actually been breastfeeding effectively for months, the odds are great that both of you have actually ended up being extremely connected to the procedure. Now, mommy has to take a medication which disrupts the breastfeeding procedure. What could be done? Before you just quit breastfeeding all at one time, it might be needed to work through the procedure thoroughly.

Can Something Else Be Done?

If you have actually been told by your physician that it is medically required to quit breastfeeding because of a medication you are taking, among the essential things to do is informing the physician about how that may not be a choice. For instance, if your kid has actually been nursing routinely and is not yet consuming a large quantity of food beyond breast milk, notify the physician. Numerous physicians are just not familiar with the baby weaning procedure and the significance of enabling the procedure to occur slowly. Learn if there is another medication which could be taken which is safe for baby. Oftentimes, this is a choice.

If you are not exactly certain if the medication you are taking is good to take during breastfeeding, it is a more effective choice to do a bit of research initially. It is common for physicians who are not sure if you ought to be breastfeeding to merely state that you shouldn't be. Do a bit of research by yourself, utilizing just dependable sources, obviously. It is typically an excellent idea to utilize the Doctor's Desk Reference for this kind of information. Additionally, you could contact your pediatrician and inquire if you are able to breastfeed, taking the prescribed medications, because they are very probable to understand whether you should or not.

There might be circumstances when you merely need to quit breastfeeding right now. It may be brought on by the baby or due to something which happens. If there is a risk to the kid, do not do it, and work on weaning the baby. In case there is a possibility of weaning the kid gradually, take this path. It ought to be quite uncommon that the circumstance requires that you need to quit breastfeeding quickly. Most of the time, it is ideal to work gradually at the procedure to assist with shielding the kid from any prospective stress factors and to stay clear of any problems on your side, as well.

Chapter 15: Why Stopping Abruptly is a Bad Idea

Certain parents decide one day that they just ought to be feeding their kid anything except breast milk. You might have spent the last couple of months of breastfeeding effectively. The issue is, you should never make the shift an abrupt one. This may do a great deal of harm to both you and your kid. Rather than pushing the scenario to take place immediately, it ought to be a steady procedure that is led not by the mom or dad yet rather by the kid themselves. This enables everyone involved to work through the procedure effectively.

The sudden baby weaning procedure does harm other moms. Initially, there is the psychological detachment which needs to be handled. Many others do not understand that their kid is really going to create so many problems when they are weaning. However, even the very best are going to go through a procedure of grief for that time lost together. However, along with this, there are other reasons why the mom is going to be jeopardized. For instance, if you quit nursing right now, your breasts are going to swell, and the end outcome is an agonizing engorging. This hurts when it occurs simultaneously. Additionally, it could get worse if you establish an infection or perhaps an abscess on your breast due to it.

While these conditions might look agonizing and unpleasant, a sudden baby weaning is going to do damage to the kid too. The initial and most substantial trauma is going to form the psychological trauma that the kid experiences. They have actually discovered this to be far more than simply their food source. They feel protected here. They are comforted by the mom's arms and their existence generally. If you take this away in a quick flash, the kid could be damaged mentally from it. You want to keep in mind that there is no method to inform your kid that it is all right since they do not totally comprehend vocal interactions at this moment.

Rather than deciding to quit nursing your kid immediately, keep in mind that the procedure could be done even more effectively if it is done slowly. This is going to enable the kid to enhance the desire to quit breastfeeding. The slow procedure additionally permits them to move a bit of of their breastfeeding attachment to other things and enables the mom's body to adapt much more to the procedure.

Chapter 16: Baby Weaning Process

How does baby weaning, in fact, take place? The procedure could be long and intricate, yet a brief version of the procedure could be explained in one word: slow. Simply put, you and your kid ought to take the procedure gradually working towards the common objective of no longer breastfeeding yet enabling the kid to rely entirely on solid foods for their sustenance. The procedure additionally includes a lot of time to work through in regards to psychological stability. You and your kid have to both be prepared for the break, and you both ought to be physically able to make the shift.

Introducing The Process

As your kid grows older, his/her stomach becomes bigger. They no longer have the ability to feel full from consuming simply breast milk. This might induce them to wish to breastfeed more frequently and gradually. You can end up being really overloaded by the procedure. This is when it ends up being time to add certain solid foods to the kid's diet plan. The majority of babies are going to begin with an intro to baby cereal, which is a product which breast milk might be included to so as to make it more appropriate to the kid. As soon as your physician states that you can present more solid foods into the kid's diet plan, have a go at it.

This is the initial step in the baby weaning procedure. As quickly as the kid starts to consume some solid foods, you are going to have to be motivated to do so. Never ever permit the kid to attempt more than one kind of brand-new food in any 3-day duration as you want to be certaain that he/she is not allergic to the food. In time, integrate meals, where the kid is consuming 3 meals of baby food paired with fewer breast sessions. You are highly probable to see that the baby is more happy to consume solid foods as they grow older.

Completing The Process

There is no easy procedure to quit breastfeeding completely. Instead, the procedure ought to be done as a gradual one, where the kid gradually begins to substitute their breast milk with solid foods. In doing that, the kid is going to end up being more familiar with consuming solid foods and is going to be less probable to be thinking about breastfeeding. Ultimately, you are going to have the ability to introduce cow's milk to the kid's diet plan as they are sufficiently old. This could be an immediate substitute for breast milk for an older kid.

Chapter 17: Time for Night Weaning

For the majority of kids, the thought of quitting any feeding might appear crazy. In case you are a breastfeeding mommy, your kid is latched on good, and he/she is probably acting as if they are starving with every feeding. How could you potentially believe the kid is prepared to be weaned from breastfeeding during the night? Regardless of why the kid is taking in these nutrients, it might be required for you to get additional sleep. There are just so many sleep-deprived night before you burn out. Because of this, it might be required to begin promoting night weaning.

By the time your kid is approximately 4 to 6 months old, they ought to be capable of taking in ample calories during the day to break the night feeding. How do you know if your kid is prepared? Their age is a great sign. Certain children are prepared prior to this, however, by this age, you could securely presume they won't go hungry. In case your kid is getting up during the night, remember that it might be since the kid's body has actually just ended up being used to waking up at that time. They might not be really getting up due to the fact that they are starving.

Are you prepared to quit night feedings? If you are succeeding with night feeding and you have the time to commit to it without it impacting your requirement for sleep and your general wellness, there must not be a rush to quit feedings during the night. Meanwhile, you wish to teach your kid to sleep properly throughout the night, and to do so, you are going to want to motivate them to sleep through it without, in fact, getting up for feedings.

Are you prepared to quit night feedings?

- Is the baby at least 4 months old?

- Is he/she taking in a great quantity of calories and nutrients throughout the day? Speak to your pediatrician to learn what is needed every day for your kid's age and size.

- Are you getting ample sleep? If not, you want to think about night weaning

In case you are still uncertain if you ought to quit night breastfeeding your kid, speak with your pediatrician about the procedure. You might be shocked to discover that your kid is prepared for the procedure, and you have the ability to get more sleep without robbing the kid.

Chapter 18: Tips For Natural Weaning

As a mom, your task is to offer the ideal to your kid. You have actually decided to enable your kid to quit breastfeeding naturally. The procedure is referred to as natural weaning, and you need to pay attention to the kid to see when he/she does not require breastfeeding any longer. This is maybe among the ideal kinds of tools offered to ladies because it enables both the parent and the kid to be in a great situation when the decision to quit takes place.

To assist you with the procedure of breastfeeding naturally, think about the following suggestions.

- Urge your kid to eat 3 full solid food meals, plus treats during the day. As the kid grows older, you are going to wish to motivate them to rely upon these meals for their nourishment instead of breastfeeding. By the age of one, kids ought to be consuming meals like this.

- Have breastfeeding as a thing separate from other meals. Breastfeed in just one place and do not urge the kid to link this location with food, yet only with breastfeeding. The less time you spend there, the less they are going to consider breastfeeding.

- Provide the kid with more time to be held and snuggling with you. You wish to motivate the kid to quit breastfeeding, however, if they are doing so due to the fact that they are hanging on to this time with you rather than utilizing it for food, they are most likely in requirement of more time with you throughout other parts of the day. Create time for you both to be near.

- You could still provide the baby weaning kid with breast milk in a cup if it enables you to assist them to feel great about the procedure. It could additionally assist you in breaking the dependence and need.

- Give the procedure time. It could require numerous months for a kid to, in fact, want to stop breastfeeding. Yet, it does not have to be something which is discussed so much as it is carried out naturally. When a kid has the ability to forget about the procedure, they feel great, and so do you regarding quitting.

Naturally, weaning your kid from the bottle is a crucial step in making it possible for that kid to establish completely. Yet, it is essential to enable the procedure to move effectively and slowly. By providing them with the say in when they have to breastfeed or not, the procedure is simpler.

Chapter 19: Night Weaning

For those moms out there all set to quit breastfeeding their kid during the night, there is hope. Obtaining a decent night's sleep suggests not needing to get up for a minimum of 6 hours per night. Anybody with a baby in the house is waiting on that day when the baby does not have to wake you up, and you could gently fall asleep in your bed. Yet, there arrives a time when you might have to work to encourage this procedure to occur. There are lots of methods to arrive at the point of night weaning. Here are certain pointers to assist you through the procedure.

1: Slow and Steady Wins The Race

It s essential to take the procedure of night weaning gradually. You wish to motivate the kid to quit the procedure slowly. An excellent procedure to begin with is to merely begin offering the kid fewer minutes at each of the breasts. This enables them to get a tinier quantity of milk.

2: Increase the Length

If your baby gets up at 2 am every day to breastfeed, you might wish to begin pushing off the time when the kid is, in fact, breastfed. Lots of parents rush in to get the procedure began so they could return to sleep. Stay clear of this when night weaning. Rather, when the baby wakes you, attempt to comfort them with patting and calming them for 10 to 15 minutes prior to enabling them to breastfeed. They might fall back asleep without having to feed, as well.

3: Provide The Kid With More Throughout The Day

Obviously, it is vital to guarantee your kid is obtaining ample nutrients during the day before beginning to wean from breastfeeding during the night. By doing this, the kid has the needed calories, and they are not starving when they get up. Kids additionally have to be motivated to quit and eat. As they age, they might stand up to eating at a scheduled time due to the fact that they wish to play. Motivate them to eat at that schedule, as it can motivate them to sleep better during the night when you do so.

Breastfeeding does not have to stop even if you are night weaning. The advantage of night weaning is that it permits the kid to, in fact, stop waking up during the night to eat. You are going to discover that this is going to allow them to have excellent sleep patterns during the remainder of their lives, as well.

Chapter 20: Weaning A Toddler If a Brand-new One Is On The Way

Moms typically need to balance 2 kids at the same time. If you are prepared to have another baby, or are pregnant, yet you have a toddler who is still nursing, this whole balancing ordeal can get slightly difficult. Besides, you want to be able to offer the baby the complete capability to nurse while still fulfilling the requirements of your toddler. While you may do both, you might discover that it is time for you to begin weaning the toddler from breastfeeding to ensure that you could begin working towards the objective of being prepared to provide for the brand-new baby.

To assist you during this procedure, here are a couple of actions. Amazingly, you might find yourself able to make this shift take place much easier than you anticipated, specifically if your toddler is at least 12 to 16 months of age.

- Motivate more cup drinking. A toddler has to know how to do this. Include cups during meals and make certain they have the ability to drink well from a cup prior to quitting breastfeeding.

- Motivate solid food eating in kids as they age, based upon your pediatrician's suggestions. You want the kid to discover how to consume all solid foods.

- Make certain to satisfy the toddler's requirements for you. Besides, they desire time with you more than they desire the breastfeeding nutrients. Hang out with the kid and snuggle with them. Having time together, such as this, without breastfeeding, is going to fulfill their psychological requirement for it.

- Get aid from daddy. He could assist the toddler in checking out brand-new foods, and if needed, he could begin bottle-feeding the kid.

- Speak with your physician about any issues you are having. The majority of kids are not going to have problems weaning, however, some might. This might be an indication of the kid not obtaining ample nutrition throughout the day.

It might be feasible for you to nurse 2 babies at once, however, this procedure could tire you out and might leave the kids battling for you simultaneously. Rather than heading down this path, you might wish to think about weaning the baby. This is feasible, and it is going to help the toddler in getting used to somebody else getting the nursing from mommy by the time the baby arrives. Providing the kid with the convenience and security he/she requires is a really vital part of the weaning procedure.

Chapter 21: What Happens When You Stop Breastfeeding?

Breastfeeding does not have to last for too long. Ultimately, your kid is going to stop breastfeeding, no matter if you are weaning them or if you are, in fact, enabling the procedure to occur naturally. Lots of ladies are dealing with the thought of what is going to occur to their breasts when they do quit breastfeeding. The idea of having soft breasts that merely droop is not a thing which is pleasing to anyone. There is no question that your breasts are going to be a little different, however, they do not always need to end up being unsightly.

There are lots of things that are going to determine what occurs to your breasts as you quit breastfeeding. Along with stopping to breastfeed, elements such as your age and your weight are going to impact this. Gravity, and even pregnancy itself, are going to impact how your breasts feel and look. Each of these things is going to indicate what is going to occur as soon as you stop breastfeeding, as well.

Throughout your pregnancy, your breasts need to get bigger so that they could accommodate the milk for the baby. Along with this bigger size, your nipples might additionally darken. Your areola might additionally darken. You might additionally discover that the nipples appear to be bigger. This is just one part of preparing for the baby. When you deliver, your breasts truly kick into gear. They will most probably feel much heavier, and you are going to observe that they appear to fill out more so. This is what occurs when your milk comes in. This generally occurs within a day or so of delivering.

Over the following couple of weeks, you might feel like as breasts are exceptionally big, however, this is going to pass. Typically, within the very first 2 to 3 weeks, the breasts are going to stay heavy like this. It is simply to guarantee that the baby has the ability to get as much as he/she requires, and it additionally enables your body to get used to the quantity of milk which is required. After these initial couple of weeks, your breasts are going to begin to get tinier and are going to remain this way up until you wean your kid.

What you might not wish to know is that your breasts are very probable to go back to their typical size, pre-pregnancy, as you wean from breastfeeding. Along with this change, you are going to discover they are not as young-looking or as lively as they once were. Nevertheless, there is no method to prevent this, unless you never ever get pregnant.

Chapter 22: Baby Weaning Explained

As a newborn's parent, all you are able to actually think about is making certain that your baby is adapting to breastfeeding well. Before you know it, however, it is time to begin considering baby weaning. This is the procedure which all mammals have to go through. Each animal which nurses has to be capable of breaking away from the procedure ultimately to enable them to shift onto solid foods and eating on their own. While numerous moms and dads fear this procedure, it could be really constructive, and it is inescapable.

Why Is It Difficult?

The natural concern which somebody from the outside might have is this: Why is baby weaning such a complicated procedure? Why is it so difficult? The procedure is frequently complicated for a variety of reasons. Initially, lots of moms and dads see breastfeeding much differently than simply feeding their kid. The bond formed during this time is something special. Plus, this is a memorable time that moms and kids get to share collectively. Yet, even beyond this, there are other reasons which make it tough. Assisting a kid to change is not constantly a dry and cut procedure. Additionally, in some cases, the kid simply does not do well at the same time.

What To Do

There is a lot to discover about the procedure of baby weaning; however, the primary step is education. Before you begin to deal with this procedure by yourself, make it your objective to comprehend the numerous techniques available. Then, pick the ones you feel most comfy utilizing. Mom and kid are not the same, so it could be tough discovering that particular approach that works for you both. Yet, it is additionally essential to bear in mind that in a lot of circumstances, baby weaning does go off without a hitch. You can have a simple shift if you are prepared for it.

Take a while to think about the numerous baby weaning approaches. Most notably, invest time in the procedure yourself. Simply put, make sure you are mentally prepared for this shift, given that, usually, it is going to be the mom that has a hard time instead of the kid. Lastly, make sure you have aid. You are going to require assistance and support along the way. The bright side is that you can get this from your kid's dad, your household, and your friends. Additionally, there are exceptional resources available online to assist you, too.

Chapter 23: Why is Weaning Hard?

If you resemble many moms and dads, you actually would love a couple of additional months of keeping your kid as a baby. However, as they grow, you need to make decisions, consisting of decisions about weaning the kid. Weaning your kid could be a challenge, but for some individuals, the challenge is more difficult than for others. What might be behind this trouble? There might be numerous things; however, it is essential for you to understand what is occurring with your kid so that you can guarantee that the kid is mentally all right with the procedure.

For those moms who are having a problem with weaning, you might wish to take a bit of additional time to find out why. Generally, a kid is going to resist to some degree, particularly if they are starving. In this instance, you are going to want to guarantee the kid is being fed appropriately and is obtaining the essential calories he/she requires. Talk with your pediatrician about the amount of calories your kid requires for their size, age and weight. As soon as you are sure they are obtaining the correct amount of calories, here are certain other things to consider when having a tough time with weaning.

1. Is your kid having a hard time since he/she is not obtaining ample time with mommy? The kid might miss this intimate time and be craving it. 2. Have there been modifications in their schedule they are not getting used to? You ought to attempt to change one thing at a time for the kid to ensure that they do not feel like they remain in consistent flux. 3. Have you returned to work? Once again, if they are not receiving their fill of mommy, they might begin attempting to breastfeed since this is a promise of love and cuddle time. 4. Is the kid ill? Some kids require convenience and "good feelings" which originates from being near to mommy when they are not feeling well. Kids that are sick are going to wish to nurse more than those who are well. 5. Observe any significant changes in your house? If so, this may be why your kid is having a hard time.

When there are no other indications that there is a problem, your kid might simply require more time. Provide the time they require. You might wish to stop attempting to breastfeed for a while, and after that, return to it in a month or so. They are going to stop breastfeeding ultimately; it simply depends upon when they are prepared to.

Chapter 24: When To Baby Wean

There are various viewpoints on when you ought to wean your kid from breastfeeding. The signs are all distinct and, in reality, you ought to consider this a procedure which is particular to you and to your kid. Every kid is really distinct in how they feel and respond to baby weaning. By many accounts, the ideal method to understand if your kid is prepared to wean is to permit the procedure to occur naturally. This is, in fact, how most moms and kids are going to go through the procedure, and it is most probably to be the ideal path for you and your kid to go through, as well.

It is optimal for your baby to just grow out of breastfeeding. This is natural weaning, often referred to as a baby-led weaning. It is necessary to understand what your baby requires, as each kid is distinct. You might discover that your kid requires more time than your initial kid to make this breastfeeding break. If you take a look at your kid's other locations of advancement, you might currently understand what the kid is going to require. For instance, some kids demand to be held more. Other kids like to play by themselves. You would not typically force a kid to establish in a different way in these other areas, which implies you actually should not do so at this moment either. It is important that you permit the kids to grow as they would naturally.

Do not establish a time for how long your kid is going to nurse. Attempt to be more versatile about the whole procedure. This procedure ought to be one which takes place as naturally as feasible so that there is no restriction or risk for either of you throughout the procedure. Do you understand what the initial step in the procedure is? The initial step is as straightforward as providing your kid with his/her initial food bites.

As you begin thinking of baby weaning, understand that this is not the initial occasion. Unlike giving that initial food bite, the procedure is not a thing which you simply choose to do one day. Instead, it is a procedure that typically takes a couple of months of adjusting and a slow-moving one. Offer your kid the capability to grow and establish as it feels appropriate to do. This eventually is going to offer you and him the ideal capability to overcome baby weaning together. Baby weaning is a delightful procedure when done so.

Chapter 25: When To Night Wean

Night weaning is a procedure which includes helping a breastfed baby to cease taking feedings during the night. Similar to bottle-fed babies, the procedure is a great one for the kid. You want the kid to sleep during the night without having to get up for a feeding. Each kid is distinct in regards to the length of time it is going to require for them to sleep through the whole night. However, it is frequently essential to take actions that move procedure along. Bear in mind that night weaning just impacts the night. The majority of moms and dads are going to wish to think about feeding their baby by breast during the day.

A kid is most probable to sleep through the night provided that they have ample calories in their system to maintain them pleased during the night. This is not a thing which the majority of kids are going to have the ability to do inside the initial weeks of their lives merely since they are too young and have stomachs which are too little. Generally, by the time a kid is 4 to 6 months old, they are taking in ample calories during the day, and they should not require feeding during the night for at least 5 to 6 hours at a time. Certain babies might have to feed for more, and certain babies are going to night wean far earlier than this.

Certain babies require feeding during the night by breast due to the fact that they require this not just for the food, but for the nearness it permits them. For instance, maybe you have actually returned to work. Your kid is now seeing you less and bonding with you less. They might get up during the night wishing to breastfeed, not since they are starving, yet most likely since the kid wants to hang on to more time with mommy. This could be a typical requirement particularly as your kid establishes mentally.

Put in the time to approach night feeding. Do not attempt to push the scenario on your kid because he/she is not probable to take to this well. Instead, they will carry on waking you up until they are pleased that they are obtaining ample attention from you. Night weaning could and ought to be taken into consideration when your kid is old enough and wants to wean. You could begin the procedure as soon as the kid reaches between 4 and 6 months of age.

I hope that you enjoyed reading through this book and that you have found it useful. If you want to share your thoughts on this book, you can do so by leaving a review on the Amazon page. Have a great rest of the day.

Printed in Great Britain
by Amazon